A *Doonesbury* Book
I Have No Son
by G. B. Trudeau

POPULAR LIBRARY • NEW YORK

I HAVE NO SON

Selected cartoons from

BUT THIS WAR HAD SUCH PROMISE

Dear Rev. Berrigan;
I've been meaning to
write you for sometime
about this Kissinger
kidnapping business. I
want to offer my services
on your second attempt.

TAP TAP

I've got this great, evil
Kidnap plan that's bound
to work. Once we get him
kidnapped, we can leave
him here at the commune
where I live. One of my
best men, Didi Robins
will guard him until the
ransom is paid.

TAP

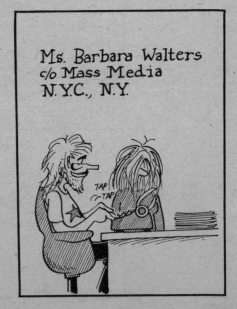

AND ESPECIALLY WITH HIS WHEAT PATCH! YOU WON'T BELIEVE WHAT HE DOES TO HIS WHEAT PATCH EVERY DAY!

TRY ME.

'MORNING, WHEAT PATCH! TIME FOR OUR SHAMPOO!

HE SO WANTED
TO BE PART
OF THE RESIDUAL
FORCE.